Original title:
Succulents and Sunbeams

Copyright © 2025 Creative Arts Management OÜ
All rights reserved.

Author: Colin Harrington
ISBN HARDBACK: 978-1-80581-779-6
ISBN PAPERBACK: 978-1-80581-306-4
ISBN EBOOK: 978-1-80581-779-6

Oasis Hues and Radiant Views

In pots of joy, the greens do thrive,
With tiny wears, they come alive.
Cacti dance with prickly flair,
While others bask without a care.

They laugh at drought, they laugh at heat,
In vibrant shades, they claim their seat.
A roly-poly, round and stout,
Winks at sunshine, no doubt about.

Warmth Inked in Leafy Designs

With patterns bold and colors bright,
They mix and match, a true delight.
Each leaf a story, wild and free,
In sunlit tones, they find their glee.

A jade brigade with joyful grins,
They poke out roots, like playful twins.
With every sip of sunshine's glow,
A happy dance they surely show.

Light's Embrace on Sturdy Leaves

A sassy plant with attitude,
Waves its arms, oh so shrewd.
It stretches high to claim the rays,
While casting shadows, mischief plays.

In pots they sit, a quirky crew,
With lots of laughs and sage to chew.
As sunlight spills on rugged skin,
They whisper secrets, chuckles begin.

Nature's Heartbeats in Glorious Light

Green pals with smiles, so sincere,
Guard the sun, their biggest cheer.
Each leaf a high-five to the sky,
As bees buzz by with wings that fly.

They grow like jokes, they sprout and twist,
In radiant realms where glee can't miss.
Each prick and pop, a giggle ensues,
In nature's smile, they spread their muse.

The Warm Embrace of Green

In pots so round, they love to stay,
Chasing sunbeams through the day.
Their leaves like pillows, soft and plump,
Creating laughter with each little bump.

A drink of water, just a splash,
They thrive on care, always a dash.
With smiles that sprout on every side,
These leafy friends are a fun-filled ride.

Blooming with Solar Energy

Lo and behold, they stretch and yawn,
Craving warmth at the break of dawn.
In the sunlight's glow, they love to wink,
   Making the world a brighter pink.

When clouds roll in and skies turn gray,
They dance and giggle in their own way.
  It's a sun-soaked party, oh so neat,
   With prickly fun beneath our feet.

Tapestry of Light and Greenery

A patchwork quilt of greens and hues,
Soft and cozy like forgotten shoes.
They chat with breezes, share some laughs,
Growing tiny treasures by the paths.

Each curious form, a quirky friend,
With nature's tools, they twist and bend.
A wealth of charm in every curl,
These jolly greens give life a whirl.

Prickled Wonders of the Heat

With playful spikes that wink and poke,
They're telling secrets, they're having a joke.
A gentle nudge can spark a cheer,
Watching them giggle as spring draws near.

In desert climes where warmth prevails,
They thrive on sun without details.
Foolish and funny, in their own zone,
Championing green in a prickly tone.

Serpents of the Sun

In pots they slither, oh so sly,
Twisting and turning, reaching high.
Caught a glimpse of my shoes, oh dear!
Are they plotting my sudden rear?

With every drizzle, they dance and sway,
Stretching their arms in a sunlit play.
If they could talk, they'd surely tease,
'You're looking a bit wilted, need some ease?'

Heartfelt Blooms in the Day's Glow

In the morning light, they puff with pride,
Next to their pals, they just can't hide.
One brave bloom winks, says with a pout,
'With me around, there's never a drought!'

And when the sun beats with all its might,
They wear their shades and laugh in delight.
'Take that, neighbor, you've got nothin' on me!
I'm the cutest in this botanical spree!'

The Elegance of Drought-born Beauty

With roots so deep, they flaunt their pride,
In a world of thirst, they just abide.
An awkward dance, all wobbly and bright,
'Look at us shine, though we lack the light!'

When clouds roll in, they start to cheer,
'Rain, oh sweet rain, we hold you dear!
But don't be hasty, we love the warm,
A sip now and then keeps us from harm!'

Emblems of Life Beneath the Haze

In shadows they lurk, with style galore,
Filling the air with whispers and lore.
The fatter they get, the funnier still,
'More snacks for me, some water to fill!'

Nudging each other, they giggle and sway,
'We're the life of this pot, come what may!
So bring on the sun, or hail the rain,
We're the champions of this leafy domain!'

Echoes of Color in the Sun's Warmth

In pots of bright laughter, they wiggle with glee,
Dressed in green frocks, a sight to see.
With sunny smiles, they dance quite bold,
Tickling the air, a joy to behold.

Each leaf has a story, quirky and fun,
Having a party, just under the sun.
They whisper secrets in playful jest,
This crew of green pals is simply the best!

Drinking up rays like a cool lemonade,
In their rich little kingdom, all worries fade.
They wiggle and giggle with radiant mirth,
Chasing away clouds, bringing good cheer to Earth.

Luminous Tales from Dry Lands

In deserts where laughter meets heat's embrace,
These little green wonders find their own space.
Telling tall tales with a wink from above,
Each one a character, full of unique love.

When the sun greets each morning with warmth and delight,
They share a quick joke, a jovial sight.
With roots that are strong, they chuckle and sway,
Making dry lands their stage for play.

With each thirsty sip, their humor awakens,
Transforming the dry with giggles and shakin's.
Their charm is contagious, a quirky delight,
In the glow of the day, they shine oh so bright.

Desert Jewels in Morning Light

Morning arrives with laughter's soft gleam,
These gems of the sand begin to beam.
With petals that shimmer in tones so bold,
They jest and they jive, a treasure untold.

Each tiny creature in its quirkiness dressed,
Recites little rhymes, always the best.
With spunky demeanor and cheeky guise,
They brighten the day, a colorful surprise!

Cacti do poetry, a prickly affair,
While giving sly winks at anyone there.
In the light of the morn, with nary a care,
They spread joy and laughter, sprinkled everywhere.

Green Guardians of the Radiant Day

Rulers of brightness, protectors of cheer,
These green little champions bring laughter near.
With swords made of leaves and smiles so wide,
They guard sunny kingdoms, full of fun pride.

In whimsical outfits of varying shades,
They plot and they plan, enjoy playful raids.
Holding court in the sun's gentle grin,
With clever banter, the jokes start to spin.

With a wiggle and jiggle, they bask in the glow,
Outsmarting the shadows with laughs left to sow.
Each moment a treasure, they twist and they play,
These green little guardians brighten the day!

Life's Luminous Emissaries

In a pot, they dance with glee,
Chasing sunlight, wild and free.
Plants in shades of green and gold,
Telling tales of warmth untold.

With tiny hats and prickly bites,
They party under meteor lights.
A cactus throws a silly shade,
While others join the leafy parade.

Their roots stretch out beneath the soil,
With whispered laughs and endless toil.
They poke each other, say, 'Oh dear!'
'Can you believe this sunny sphere?'

When rain comes down, they cheer in joy,
A splashy gift, oh what a ploy!
With every drop, they grow so tall,
Nature's pranksters, one and all.

A Patchwork of Light and Green

In pots adorned like patchwork quilts,
They sip the sun while bouncing wilts.
A rosette nudges close to bloom,
'Watch out!' it grins, 'I've got room!'

One leaf declares, 'I'm more than tough!'
Another says, 'You're just too gruff!'
They swap their jokes, exchange their quips,
With happy hearts, not one eclipse.

When twilight spreads its golden hue,
These leafy jesters plot anew.
They strategize on gaining light,
'Let's stretch out further, quite the sight!'

At nightfall, when the stars peek in,
They giggle softly, full of grin.
A leafy chat beneath the moon,
A patchwork life, oh what a tune!

Arid Wonders Awash in Sunlight

In sandy beds, they sprout and dream,
Their smiles wide, a sunlit beam.
With foes like drought and hungry pests,
They tackle woes with funny quests.

A sagebrush winks, 'Is that a fly?'
A tuber shouts, 'Just let it try!'
With sun hats made of petals bright,
They stand in rows, a silly sight.

The heatwave makes them shiver cool,
They giggle 'round the sunny pool.
With every ray of laughter shared,
They conquer heat, none left impaired.

As twilight falls and shadows grow,
They take a bow for the warm glow.
These wonders bask in night's embrace,
A jolly crew in this wild space.

The Luster of Leafy Companionship

A group of greens with quirky charms,
In porcelain homes, they sound alarms.
'Is that a window? Light's coming through!'
They stretch and reach, each bid adieu.

One pushy leaf, 'Hey look at me!'
Waving wildly, full of glee.
While others laugh, 'You always show!'
A competition in the glow.

Together they sip on golden rays,
Sharing secrets of the sun's plays.
In their pot, they plot and scheme,
A leafy band, a sunny dream.

And when the moon decides to rise,
They gather round for starlit sighs.
With roots entwined, they share the night,
In leafy bonds, all feels just right.

Desert Dwellers in Sunlight

Little plants on sandy ground,
Dancing with the sun around.
With a grin, they soak the rays,
Making funny faces all day.

Bouncing gently in the breeze,
These green pals do as they please.
Drinking water like it's juice,
Living life with no excuse.

Under the Glare of Golden Rays

Under sunny skies so bright,
Cacti wear their hats so tight.
Each wears spikes like fashion trends,
Hoping that the fun never ends.

With giggles, they twist and sway,
Shading friends from light's ballet.
In the glow, their colors pop,
Wiggling to the disco sup.

Thorny Companions Embrace the Light

Friends with spikes and prickly flair,
Crack jokes without a single care.
In bright warmth, they love to tease,
A secret club among the leaves.

Doing their best to look quite cool,
Playing tricks, that's their rule.
Cactus parties in the sun,
Prickly fun for everyone!

Green Gems of the Arid Land

In the dust, they shine so bright,
Green gems in the fading light.
Sipping sun in every glance,
They're always up for a dance.

With tiny smiles, they plot and play,
Winking at the sun's ballet.
Life's a laugh in dry terrain,
A wild party with no rain!

Bottled Sunshine within Green Walls

In pots so round, they dance and sway,
With faces bright, they greet the day.
A cactus sneezes, oh what a sight,
While succor blooms, feeling just right.

They sip their drinks from droplets rare,
While plotting escapes from their green chair.
A tumble here, a twisty bloom,
In this quirky jungle, there's always room.

Let's not forget the potted jokes,
When leafy pals start to poke.
They giggle in silence, thrive in glee,
In little worlds, just them and me.

Though sunlight glows and shadows play,
These green wonders brighten every day.
With laughter shared, their spirits soar,
In this sunny realm, we crave for more.

The Golden Touch of Nature's Kindness

With golden rays that paint the leaves,
Each plant concedes what it believes.
A rose quips, "I bloom with flair!"
While daisies flirt, without a care.

The mint sprigs dance in breezy tunes,
While thyme complains about the loons.
"Too much sun!" grumbles sleepy sage,
As lavender laughs, the seasoned sage.

In this garden of witty dreams,
The sunlight drips with teasing beams.
Plants trade quips; who knows their fate?
"Just keep me watered, then seal my fate!"

Oh nurturing hands, come close and stay,
With your funny ways, brighten my day.
Nature's touch is sprightly and wild,
A golden family, forever beguiled.

Potted Radiance in Abundance

With pots galore stacked high and low,
The cheeky greens put on a show.
A jade plant jives with wavy curls,
While little ones whirl, mimicking twirls.

In a sunny nook, they chime and cheer,
Whispering secrets, loud and clear.
"I'm not thirsty, just a little dry!"
And smiles erupt as they sigh and lie.

Tiny pots laugh, oh what a crew!
With twinkling leaves in vibrant hue.
They soak up giggles, bask in fun,
Throwing shade at the bright yellow sun.

Bound by laughter, they sparkle bright,
This potted party feels just right.
Each day they toast to growth and glee,
In cheerful company, wild and free.

Daring to Thrive in Dryness

In cozy nooks, they call to play,
These daring greens in a sun-drenched bay.
With roots that dig for treasure deep,
While jokes abound, their secrets keep.

In dusty corners, they take a stand,
A rogue little sprout with a cunning plan.
"Water? Nah! Who needs that fuss?"
As onlookers marvel in verdant trust.

With drooping leaves, they wave goodnight,
While swaying softly in the soft moonlight.
They giggle and plot their grand escape,
"Tomorrow's sun, we'll reshape!"

Daring to thrive, these plants do cheer,
Embracing oddities, far and near.
With humor and light, they stretch and strive,
In a dry world, they truly thrive.

Lush Lifestyles Under Solar Kisses

In pots adorned with vibrant hues,
They lounge and sip on sun-infused brews.
With cheeky hopes, they soak up rays,
Playing hide and seek in sunny bays.

Their leaves are thick, with tales to share,
In bright attire, they bask and dare.
"What's a little heat?" they giggle, sing,
While dodging bugs that buzz and cling.

With roots that twist like a dancer's twirl,
In every corner, they spin and whirl.
They frolic lightly on the warm, dry earth,
A jolly crowd, declaring mirth.

Cacti crack jokes in a prickly way,
"Don't poke fun, we thrive in the fray!"
Underneath the sun's bright, teasing beams,
Life's a party, or so it seems.

Prickly Embrace of Warmth

In the heat, they stand so bold,
August tales of joy unfold.
With spines adorned, they're quite the show,
Hug them tight, if you dare to go slow.

They wink and nod, a sassy crew,
"Keep your distance, but we like you!"
Rubbing shoulders with a sun-drenched friend,
In their prickly charm, all rules bend.

"Oh, watch your step!" one quips on cue,
"Landing here could be quite askew!"
Yet laughter echoes, bright and free,
In the warmth, they thrive with glee.

Life's a cactus dance under bright skies,
With every poke, we improvise.
In sunny hugs, they find their grace,
With cheeky laughter on each face.

Sunlit Trinkets of Resilience

Little gems of vibrant green,
Dancing wildly, a curious scene.
Every pot a treasure chest,
With sunshine shining, they feel blessed.

Twirling leaves like they've got flair,
They claim the light with style and care.
"Who needs water when sun's this fun?"
They quip as they bask, each one a pun.

In the glow, they settle with glee,
"Shade is nice, but we love to be free!"
Each leaf a badge of a glorious fight,
In a world so bright, they own the light.

With winds that sing and twirl around,
Their laughter echoes, a joyous sound.
"Join the party!" they call out loud,
In their little corner, they're oh so proud.

Verdant Whispers in Golden Glow

In the hush of the golden beam,
They whisper secrets, live the dream.
"Did you hear what the aloe said?"
"It's chill; it just snoozes in its bed!"

With leaves that stretch and tease the sun,
In playful banter, they have their fun.
"Who needs a drink? Let's toast the day!"
"Cheers to warmth, come what may!"

They sway and chuckle, a leafy crowd,
"Feeling bold, let's sing out loud!"
For every day's a chance to play,
In this leafy life, they never sway.

Underneath a bright and cheerful dome,
In sunlit joy, this is their home.
With laughter echoing soft and sweet,
Life's a comedy, and they can't be beat.

Petals and Sunshine in Harmony

Tiny green thrones, they sit with pride,
Absorbing sunlight, their joy won't hide.
They laugh at weeds, those pesky little foes,
In a game of growing, anything goes!

With wrinkled leaves, they make their stand,
Winking at cacti across the land.
In pots and gardens, they cheer with glee,
Welcome to our wacky, sunny spree!

Guardians of the Glistening Light

In a world of sunshine, they strike a pose,
Staring down shadows that try to impose.
With pride, they sway in a breeze so light,
Chasing away gloom like a funny sight!

Each leaf a giggle, each flower a cheer,
They shout, "More sunlight! We thrive right here!"
Defenders of joy with a quirky charm,
Who knew that plants could disarm with calm?

Sunstruck Spirits in Nature's Hand

When the sunbeams dance, it's a wild spree,
Bouncing like kids, as happy as can be.
They sway and twirl, in a pot they prance,
Chasing their shadows, it's a bright romance!

With petals like confetti, they throw a bash,
A fiesta of colors in a vibrant splash.
"Catch me if you can!" is their playful song,
In the garden party, where joys belong!

Flora Painting with Light

With brushes of green, they color the air,
Each beam of brilliance, beyond compare.
In a canvas of soil, they spread their cheer,
Whispering secrets to adventurers near!

Their artwork glimmers, a hilarious sight,
Painted in laughter, from morning till night.
"Can I be your muse?" one cheekily claims,
In this gallery of nature, nothing's the same!

Treading Lightly on Spiky Throne

In the kingdom of prickly spikes,
I tiptoe where mischief strikes.
The royal guards are plants gone mad,
Yet their throne is cozy, not so bad.

I dance with grace upon the scene,
A jester in the garden green.
Beware the pointy, sharp brigade,
They giggle softly, never fade.

Nature's Light Keepers

They bask in rays, a quirky crew,
With coats of green and dews so blue.
Chasing shadows, they prance around,
In laughter's glow, they can be found.

A cactus tries to steal the show,
With puns that only plants can know.
Their jokes are sharp, their humor sweet,
In nature's light, they find their beat.

Threads of Green in Sun's Embrace

In a tapestry of soft daylight,
They stretch their limbs in joyous flight.
Spindly arms with laughter weave,
Tickling clouds that never leave.

A chortle echoes through the leaves,
As dandelions play tricks with thieves.
Sun-kissed jokes on breezes dance,
In this green land, they take their chance.

The Flora of Forgotten Lands

In realms where laughter fades away,
The plants have secrets they will say.
With whispered puns and cheeky grins,
They plot their mischief, fun begins.

Among the ruins, nature's jest,
A flower shows it knows the best.
While shadows loom with curious eyes,
These plants just giggle 'neath the skies.

Cacti Dreams Under Cloudless Skies

In a garden full of prickly friends,
They talk of sunshine that never ends.
'Watch our growth,' they say with glee,
While plotting to steal my iced tea.

With a smile and a poke, they wave their thorns,
Daring any breeze that softly scorns.
'We're the coolest plants,' they boast with pride,
But they can't even dress in a leafy hide!

In a desperate moment, one fell right down,
Trying to look like a flourishing crown.
But with a thud and a twist, they lay on the ground,
A cactus ballet that knows no bound.

As they sunbathe with roots all splayed,
Plotting new pranks, no shade displayed.
In laughter and mirth, they share the scene,
Cacti dreams where folly reigns supreme.

Photogenic Persuasions

With filters of sunlight and pots of clay,
Every plant poses, 'Aren't we cute today?'
Click, click, click, it's a photo shoot,
Even the weeds want a chance to be cute.

One little petal, full of sass,
Claims it's the star, while making a pass.
'Look at my bloom and my lovely shade,
Fame's just around, so don't be afraid!'

The ivy gazes with envy so bright,
'Who needs a lens when you're not polite?'
While succumbing to vivid envy's sway,
The art of relaxation is thrown away.

As lights flash and laughter spills,
Even the thorns are wearing frills.
In this world of vine-clad charms,
Every plant poses with quirky arms.

Verdant Harmonies in the Sun

Beneath the blazing orb so grand,
A quirky bunch forms a singing band.
Each leaf a note, each bloom a cheer,
Melodies spreading far and near.

The tall ones croon, with voices so wide,
While tiny buds sway from side to side.
Purling rhythms in the summer air,
With cactus beats that dance everywhere.

But wait! A gopher steals the show,
Twisting the lyrics, making them flow.
'Keep it down!' the sunflowers grin,
While rocky-faced friends request to join in.

With a twist and a turn, they each do their best,
In this sunny concert, they never rest.
Prickly, leafy, they sing with delight,
In verdant harmonies under sunlight.

Radiant Reflections in Earthy Hues

On a windowsill, so bright and spry,
Plants compete in a cheeky high-brow spy.
'Check out my color, it's dazzling and bold!'
While the shy moss looks quietly old.

With whispers of green and hues of clay,
They strut their stuff in a leafy ballet.
'Who knew I could shimmer?' said one proud sprout,
While plotting a mischief that's without doubt.

The shadows dance where the sunlight lies,
Echoes of laughter, no need for disguise.
'Earthy hues are the trend,' they cheerfully shout,
With roots entwined, there's no hint of doubt.

In this patch of glory, they mimic the breeze,
With glances and winks, oh what a tease!
Radiant reflections, never a fuss,
Plants laughing together, joy's voluminous.

Petals of Persistence Amidst Warmth

In a pot, a cactus stood tall,
Waving its spikes like a tiny wall.
The sun said, "Come out, enjoy the day!"
"Only if you promise not to fry me away!"

A little jade plant danced with glee,
Shouting, "Look at me, I'm the queen bee!"
Her friends rolled their eyes, quite aloof,
"You're not the star, just a leafy goof!"

In a sunny corner, a string of pearls,
Swayed and shimmered, giving twirls.
"I'm cooler than all of you, can't you see?"
"Cooler? You just need more water, wee!"

They share their jokes and sunny love,
Basking in giggles, like stars above.
In the warmth, they thrive, it seems to be,
That patience and laughter are the best decree!

The Art of Green under Solar Brushstrokes

A cheery fool, a bold fern did shout,
"I'm the Picasso of plants, without doubt!"
With fronds all wild, it posed with flair,
While a sage nearby just gave a stare.

Cacti cracked wise about staying dry,
"Why get wet? Not I, oh no, not I!"
But a poor little sprout tripped on its root,
"Help, I'm just trying to look cute!"

A succulent spreading rumors of green,
"I stretch out my arms, am I too keen?"
The others snickered, with tiny grins,
"Arm-waving plants never truly win!"

Under sun's watchful, giggling rays,
Each leaf shares joys in quirky ways.
So here they bloom, under the sun's tease,
Turning the garden into pure, green ease!

Enchanted Leaves in Day's Light

A little leaf whispered, 'Oh, look at me!'
'I'm the fairest plant, can't you see?'
While a nearby aloe raised an eye,
'You're cute, but darling, don't be shy!'

The sunlight sparkled on dewy sprays,
Each flower boasting of bright, fun days.
They chirped and chirped, like birds in flight,
'How much do we love this dazzling light?'

A tip-top bloom with flair and pride,
Declared, 'I'm bright, you can't deny!'
But the shadows whispered back with cheer,
'It's okay, we love you even here!'

Together they twinkle, giggles in green,
In this sunny kingdom, they reign supreme.
With laughter and love, tall and stout,
They know the secret of fun, without a doubt!

Resilient Roots in Radiant Spaces

In pots of laughter, roots intertwine,
Living their lives, all quite divine.
One root burbled, 'I'm staying put!'
While others danced, left and right foot!

A rosette crowed about its fine shape,
'Look at me, I'm the perfect grape!'
But a tiny sprout with a wink and glee,
Said, 'You're cute, but hold your leafy spree!'

In radiant spaces, they bask and gawk,
Trading stories, having a walk.
Each leaf chuckles under bright skies,
Happiness shines in joyful cries!

Through sunny smiles, they know their way,
With roots of humor, they seize the day.
In every giggle, they find their place,
A garden of grins, full of warm embrace!

Cacti Dreams at Dawn's Awakening

In the morn when light does creep,
Spiky friends wake from their sleep.
Poking fun at passing bees,
"Not a flower, just add cheese!"

Rolling over, one pricks a toe,
"Hey buddy, don't move so slow!"
Sunshine tickles with a grin,
Cacti laugh, the day begins.

With arms raised high, they say with glee,
"We're the best, can't you see?"
Green and sharp, with a twisty flair,
Who needs water? We don't care!

In the garden, mischief brews,
Prickly jokes, with no bad news.
Cacti dreams as bright as morn,
Laughing bright from dusk till dawn.

Radiant Flora in Nature's Embrace

In a patch where giggles grow,
Plants decide to steal the show.
Waving leaves in a dance so bold,
"Splash some paint, let's break the mold!"

A daisy said with gentle cheer,
"Let's wear hats and spread some cheer!"
Sunflowers chimed in, quite sincere,
"We'll be the stars, oh dear, oh dear!"

The garden's stage is set to play,
With blooms that laugh throughout the day.
"Who needs shade when we can shine?
With glitter sprinkles, we'll be divine!"

Petals twirling, a vibrant race,
Nature's embrace, a silly space.
Color meets humor, oh what a sight,
In this garden, everything feels right!

Hues of Harmony Beneath the Sky

Underneath the azure dome,
Colorful crew feel right at home.
Daisies dressed in polka dots,
Say, "We're cooler than big shots!"

With green mustaches and silly hats,
They play tag with the buzzing gnats.
Roses blush, "We're the best in bloom!"
But then trip and land with a boom!

The sun winks at this funny show,
As petals fall like confetti, whoa!
In this wild paintbox, laughter flows,
In a world where whimsy grows.

Beneath the sky so pure and bright,
Jokes bloom like flowers, pure delight.
Colors mingle in playful spree,
A harmonious dance, oh can't you see?

Glimmering Gems on Earth's Canvas

On a hillside, shiny rocks play,
Laughing gems light up the day.
"Is it lunchtime or a joke?"
As the sparkle starts to stoke!

Stones chat in dazzling array,
"Let's form a band and sing hooray!"
Crisp clear notes on the breeze do rise,
As the shy boulders start to sing prize.

"Who's the fairest of them all?"
Rocks reply, "We stand tall!"
With each glimmer, a smile appears,
"Happiness is free, no tears!"

So nature's canvas, filled with glee,
Is where laughter flows so free.
With shining gems and joyous grace,
Earth's fun side, a happy place!

A Tapestry of Green Beneath the Sun

In a pot they dance, so spry,
With spiky hats reaching high.
They sip on water, just a sip,
Yet never seem to lose their grip.

Their leaves like little jade balloons,
Catching rays from smiling moons.
A sunbeam slides, a cheeky tease,
And they respond with a gentle breeze.

Each morning's glow, a quirky show,
These green pals put on quite a glow.
They poke and prod, they twist and bend,
A playful life that seems to mend.

Oh how they love the sunny tease,
Dancing on the gentle breeze.
In cozy pots, they plot and scheme,
Living life like a wild dream.

Shadows and Silhouettes in Bright Harmony

In the garden, shadows play,
They stretch and wiggle throughout the day.
With each stretch, down they sway,
As sunlight giggles along the way.

Their shapes resemble a funny crew,
A thousand dances, each one new.
Watch them change, it's quite the sight,
A shadow show, in pure delight.

With each blink, the light does spin,
These leafy pals play hide and grin.
They tease the light, they tease the dark,
Creating laughter in the park.

A cheerful bunch, they light the scene,
In leafy greens, they reign supreme.
To rib the sun is quite the game,
And every leaf has earned its fame.

Reveries of Resilience at Day's Zenith

At noon they shine with cheeky flair,
Defying odds with leafy care.
With hues so bright, they mock the heat,
In sunlit rooms, they find their seat.

You'd think they'd melt, but look and see,
They laugh and stand so proudly.
Each drop of water, a wild jubilee,
Their laughter echoes, "Come join me!"

When breezes tease and tremors shake,
They dip and weave, for goodness' sake.
These tough little critters know the score,
With every poke, they ask for more.

So raise a glass to these green charms,
Who weather storms with quirky arms.
Their bubbly wit will always shine,
In the grandest garden, they're divine!

Illuminated Serenity of Earth's Wonders

In pots of joy, they take a stand,
With laughter bright as grains of sand.
As sunlight beams, they come alive,
In joyous forms, they'll always thrive.

Each leaf's a tickle, soft and sly,
In brilliant hues that catch the eye.
They whisper secrets to the breeze,
A funny tale of sunlit pleas.

With careful roots, they seek the chuckle,
Their jests bounced back, a giddy shuffle.
In nature's lap, they reign as jesters,
Crafting tales while the sun lusters.

So join their dance, embrace the cheer,
In a world of green, let's all draw near.
For laughter thrives where plants convene,
Life's merry song, forever green.

Light-Kissed Cacti Tales

In a sunny spot, they stand with pride,
Poking out jokes, with nothing to hide.
Needles like humor, sharp yet sweet,
Laughing together, they can't be beat.

They whisper to the passing bees,
'Don't mind the prickles, just take your ease!'
Dancing in breezes, their arms raised high,
Sharing their stories beneath the blue sky.

When night falls down, they crack a grin,
Making the moonlight their new best friend.
A gathering of grins in the garden fair,
With every chuckle, a twinkle in the air.

So here's to the plants, with humor so grand,
Kissing the sunshine, yes, isn't it bland?
Secrets shared beneath the sun's glow,
In the land of green, the laughter will flow.

Silent Patrons of Warmth

In the corner, they sit and watch,
Guarding their soil, what a funny lot!
With tender arms and a spikes' bold flare,
They wave to the sun, without a care.

When shadows creep, they all just grin,
'Hello, dear sun, let the fun begin!'
They soak up rays like a keen-eyed cat,
Basking in warmth, how about that?

With a quirk of their stems, they make some shade,
'Stop by anytime, we've games to trade!'
Eavesdropping on flowers, with glee they lean,
Patrons of warmth, in their leafy green.

At dusk, they'll gather for stories to share,
Of bright sunny days and the friends who dare,
With prickle and cheer, they hold a feast,
In silence they thrive, living as the least.

Dappled Shadows on Prickly Skin

Behind the window, a sly one peeks,
With spiky exterior, they play hide and seek.
Casting their shadows on the floor so bright,
Dancing in laughter when no one's in sight.

'Who needs a hug? Not us!' they tease,
'Our glow is our warmth, we aim to please!'
With dappled translucence, they chuckle and sway,
In their prickly embrace, love finds its way.

When the sun comes back to tickle their skin,
They rustle their leaves and let the games begin.
With rays of affection, they bask in the light,
Shadows twist funny, the scene feels just right.

So gather round, the laughter swells,
For under the sun, each story tells,
Of dappled shadows and a prickly grin,
Life's fragility found where the fun begins.

Sunlit Serenity in a Pot

Planted in pots, they live life small,
But oh, what a show, when the sun starts to call!
Wiggly roots and tops in a dance,
Each blushing petal says, 'Take a chance!'

In the bright light, they wiggle and sway,
Making up songs that brighten the day.
'Join us dear friend, in our timeless spree,'
With pots full of cheer, it's a sight to see!

With tipsy leaves and a glimmering shine,
They plan wild tales from their tiny shrine.
'We might be small, but we're funny and spry,
And with every glance, we'll make laughs fly high!'

So here's to the flora with bright, silly charm,
Warming the hearts with their playful farm.
Sunlit serenity, in every small plot,
Life is a joke, who says it's not?

Radiance Wrapped in Verdant Vigor

In pots they dance, a leafy crowd,
Laughing at clouds, feeling quite proud.
With their plump forms so shamelessly bold,
They drink sunlight like stories untold.

A cactus in shades of cheerful glee,
Tickles the toes of a bumblebee.
While a jade plant begins to sway,
Whispering secrets of the sunny day.

Plenty of green, with humor to spare,
Winking at gardeners fumbling with care.
Their prickly charm causes quite a scene,
Who knew plants could be so downright mean?

So gather the greens, let laughter thrive,
In this silly garden, they come alive.
With a light heart and a big watering can,
Join in the fun, oh yes, if you can!

Dreams Grounded in Heat and Green

In sandy beds, where warmth does cling,
Dreams sprout forth, like a silly spring.
A portly plant in a sunhat grand,
Thinks it's a star, in command of the land.

Mocking the weeds with a leafy grin,
These little warriors know they'll win.
With each drop of sweat, they strut and sway,
Showing off flair in a sun-drenched way.

They bask and bloom, in sun's embrace,
Listening closely to the grasshopper's bass.
As butterflies flirt, all flutter and flit,
The green brigade laughs, 'We're the perfect fit!'

So here's to the dreams that sprout from the ground,
With humor and heat, the best friends we've found.
They giggle and sway, in warm summer air,
Nature's own jesters, without a care!

Nature's Palette of Light and Life

In a riot of shades, the greens prepare,
To burst forth in laughter, with colors to share.
A quirky fern, with curls so neat,
Mocks the dandelions, claiming defeat.

With a wink of a leaf and a twist of a sprout,
They hold a parade, twisting about.
A zesty zing of zest, like lime,
In this merry green carnival, it's party time!

Drawing in sunlight with a bold little pose,
Basking in warmth, while everybody knows,
A succulent's secret is fun and quite bright,
Always up for a giggle, under the light.

So paint me the landscape, where green meets the sun,
Where laughter blooms wide, and worries are done.
In nature's wildness, let's twist and twine,
In this colorful chaos, our spirits align!

Festooned in Flora Beneath the Sun

In jungles of jade, mischief does bloom,
Each plant with its humor, banishing gloom.
A lopsided leaf with a wink and a nod,
Sways to the tune of a happy little God.

In shadows they giggle, while sunbeams prance,
Holding a party, a leafy romance.
Dancing in circles, their roots intertwined,
A leafy jamboree that's one of a kind.

With bold chubby cheeks, redder than blush,
They share joyful tales in a whimsical hush.
An agave declares with pride and delight,
"I'm the life of the garden, be it day or night!"

So let's raise our pots to this funny green crew,
For every bright day, they call out, 'Woo-hoo!'
With laughter and light, in the soft afternoon,
These festive green wonders will always make room!

Resilient Greenholds of Radiance

In pots they sit, so proud and spry,
Defying drought, oh me, oh my!
They giggle at rain and dance in the glare,
Poking fun at the plants that despair.

With hues so bright, they steal the show,
Holding a party in the sun's warm glow.
You say 'water' and they shake their heads,
Just give us some light, they say, in their beds.

Each leaf a tale of joy and glee,
Chasing shadows with a cheeky spree.
They wink with pride at the thirsty bloom,
Laughing and lounging within their room.

So if your garden looks a bit bare,
Add a few greens with debonair flair.
Watch them thrive with a snicker and cheer,
In their world of fun, they've nothing to fear.

Whispers of the Sunlit Garden

In a patch of light where the laughter beams,
Chubby green fellows plot their schemes.
"Who needs water?" they proudly exclaim,
As they soak up sun, playing their game.

A cactus with style, a gallant chap,
Claims he's a pillow for the afternoon nap.
With spikes for style and no need for fuss,
He sways with a wiggle; it's all quite a plus!

Tiny rosettes in a dance so bright,
Twisting and twirling, oh what a sight!
"Bring on the drought!" they cheerfully shout,
While others fret, they're full of clout.

So here's to the crew of the laughing greens,
With cheeky smiles and quirks like means.
In their sunny realm, they're kings and queens,
Dancing to nature's simplest routines.

Oasis of Verdant Dreams

Nestled in pots, they're the jesters of green,
Winking at sunshine, a comic routine.
"Water's for flowers," they giggle with glee,
"Give us some sun, and we'll party for free!"

Bright little darlings with shapes so odd,
Laugh at the raindrops, it seems quite flawed.
They stretch in the sun with a wink and a grin,
"Come join us, friend, in our sunscreen skin!"

The succulent crew throws shade in their way,
"Beep! Beep!" they say, to the thirsty array.
Prickly and fluffy, they strut on the scene,
Bringing the fun to the spaces between.

So if you feel down, just take a quick glance,
At these leafy wonders ready to dance.
In this verdant oasis, your worries will fade,
As laughter erupts in the sun's warm cascade.

Nature's Radiant Collection

In the garden of giggles, they love to bloom,
Cheeky green warriors chase away gloom.
With plump little forms and colors so bright,
They bask in the glory of midday light.

"Water? No thanks!" they say with a laugh,
"We thrive on the sun, it's our better half!"
Producing a chuckle, they pucker and sway,
As they soak in the rays, having fun all day.

A potted brigade with quirky appeal,
Spreading joy and laughter, that's their deal.
"Chase the clouds, hail the sun!" they declare,
As they tease the day with their silly flair.

So if your spirits need a little lift,
Seek out these greens, nature's own gift.
With a sprinkle of laughter and sunlight galore,
You'll find a collection worth cherishing more.

Garden Tales Under Bright Canopies

In the garden, plants sit tight,
Wearing capes of green, what a sight!
They whisper secrets in the breeze,
Cracking jokes like playful tease.

A dandelion in a bow tie,
Claims he's the star, oh my oh my!
With petals pointing to the sky,
He dances 'round as bees fly by.

Snails in slow-motion, what a race,
They slide on trails with such grace.
One forgot to wear a shoe,
Now he's wishing for a crew.

The daisies giggle, very loud,
When a cat pops in, oh so proud.
She trips on roots, what a flop!
The laughter rings and doesn't stop.

The Poetry of Green Undercurrents

In shades of green, mischief dwells,
Where every leaf has funny tales.
A cactus dreams of being soft,
But pricks his pals, they scoff and scoff.

The sunbeams play a game of tag,
With wandering vines on a jag.
'Catch us if you can!' they shout,
As laughter echoes all about.

A row of pots has coffee chats,
Discussing shoes and fancy hats.
They wonder if they'll grow some hands,
To plant themselves in distant lands!

While ladybugs read mystery plots,
The gardener spills paint on his pots.
Colors swirl in chaotic glee,
Creating art by accident, you see.

Etchings of Light on Leafy Dreams

Under sunlight's goofy grin,
Plants hold a party to begin.
A fern in shades of emerald green,
Buys a cake, makes a scene!

The pot forgot its birthday gift,
But in a twist, spirits uplift.
A flower prances with delight,
'Though late, we'll party all night!'

Bugs in tuxedos, quite a sight,
Gather 'round for a fancy bite.
They toast to thyme; what a cheer!
Dance like no one's watching near.

Through the petals, joy erupts,
With little beetles doing jumps.
Each leaf a canvas, colors bloom,
In the wild dance of life, they zoom!

In Praise of Resilient Flora

In pots of humor, they reside,
A gang of plants with leafy pride.
'Watch us thrive!' the succulents say,
'Even when it rains, we play!'

Among the rocks, the weeds decree,
'We're the messengers, you see!'
While roots hold conference underground,
They swap the best of funny sound.

A monkey tail swings from a wall,
Yelling, 'I'll catch you all!
Don't forget me when you grow,
In this giggle fest, I'll steal the show!'

With every sprout, a giggle grows,
In vibrant hues, the garden glows.
So here's to laughter, roots, and leaves,
The patch of joy that nature weaves!

The Allure of Leafy Luminescence

In pots they sit, acting all coy,
With spiky charms, they bring us joy.
Each green delight asks for a sip,
Who knew they'd plot a green-thumb trip?

They wiggle and jive with roots so grand,
Demanding water like a diva band.
With tiny blooms that wink and sway,
It's hard to keep them at bay!

Watch them sunbathe in bright delight,
While I'm inside, avoiding daylight.
They bask and glow, like stars in bloom,
As I just trip over my broom!

Oh, leafy friends, what plots you weave!
In your green world, I just believe.
But watch your toes, I'm on a roll,
I might just dance, 'til I lose control!

Whispering Shadows Clothed in Green

In the corner, they quietly plot,
To overtake my cozy spot.
With leafy whispers and silly smirks,
They plan grand schemes in their quirky quirks.

They wink with dew in the morning sun,
As I ask myself, "What have I done?"
With each little leaf, they laugh away,
While I struggle with my indoor bouquet.

Lurking shadows with a hint of glee,
Remind me that they outsmart me.
A secret language of planty chats,
While I'm busy chasing after my cats!

Yet, I cherish their leafy parade,
Even when they join the leafy charade.
Together we groove in our quirky home,
As they sprout jokes and I just groan!

Flourish in the Embrace of the Sun

Oh, playful greens, soaking rays bright,
You stretch your limbs in sheer delight.
With every glow, you seem to cheer,
While I sip coffee, feeling austere.

They bloom and grow with a cheeky grin,
As I wrestle with my morning skin.
"Join the fiesta!" they seem to call,
But I'm still in my pajamas, that's all!

"More light!" they shout with leafy glee,
While I just wish for a warm cup of tea.
Each day a sunlit riot unfolds,
Plant-based laughter, a tale retold!

So here's to plants who snag all the rays,
With their sunny antics that truly amaze.
In this game of sunlight and chatter,
I just laugh as I sputter and stutter!

Botanicals Awakening in the Light

When dawn breaks, they rise with flair,
These cheeky greens, no time to spare.
They yawn and stretch, what a sight!
As I embrace my pillow tight.

With twisted tendrils, they plant their stake,
"Wake up, sleepyhead!" they surely take.
With bright-eyed looks and jovial cries,
They poke fun at my bleary eyes.

In their world of laughter and play,
They embark on adventures each bright day.
As I battle snoozes within my lair,
They flourish boldly, without a care!

So here they dance—a leafy parade,
While I clumsily join, feeling dismayed.
But in this chaos and morning haze,
It's hard not to giggle at their leafy ways!

Prism of Greens Under Blue Skies

In pots of joy, the greens all sway,
Their chubby forms brightening the day.
They giggle softly in the light,
With leaves like laughter, such a sight!

A cactus wearing a tiny hat,
Sips on water, how quite the spat!
A jade plant cracks a joke or two,
While sunbeams dance and join the crew!

Each prickly friend with tales to tell,
Of sunlit days where all is well.
They bask and bloom, no cares to mold,
In warmth and smiles, their secrets unfold.

With shades of green, they flirt and tease,
Luring bees with joyous ease.
In this garden of giggles, life's a play,
Where every leaf has something to say.

Sunscapes of Resilience

Little petals in a sunlit show,
They stretch and twist, and oh, how they grow!
Cacti waving, cheering for attention,
In botanical antics, they're a sensation!

Their leaves are plump, like jellybeans,
Wobbling around with giggly scenes.
They thrive and laugh through droughts and heat,
A silly band of friends, oh what a treat!

With roots that grip like they're on a spree,
They shout, "Don't water, we're wild and free!"
In sunny corners, they hold their reign,
Each telling tales of whimsical gain.

Through every season, they wear a grin,
For in their world, the fun won't thin.
The landscape sparkles in cheerful light,
As each green friend joins the good-time flight.

Chasing Sunrays in a Leafy World

In a leafy land of giggles and glee,
Local plants hang out to sip their tea.
With every sunray, they shimmy and shake,
Joking about how much water they'll take!

The aloe winks with a glimmer of sly,
"Hey, don't be shy, come bask, oh my!"
While the fern fans out with a flutter and flair,
Drawing in sunbeams like they're a rare affair!

"A little too hot!" the fan leaf squeals,
As they play tag, dodging hot sun meals.
Roots take a leap, making the earth giggle,
While sunlight drips down with a warm, happy wiggle.

With laughter echoing under the blue,
Every little leaf feels the joy anew.
This is their stage, where antics unfurl,
In a leafy world, it's a fabulous whirl!

Nature's Resilient Brightness

Amidst the rocks, a green brigade thrives,
With squishy faces, they wiggle and jive.
They chuckle at shadows, bring light so bold,
In this quirky realm, there's laughter untold!

A prickly friend with a cheeky grin,
"More sun, more fun!"—let the games begin!
Leaves do a dance, shining bright and wise,
As the sun peeks down from the wide blue skies.

"Don't mind the rain, nothing to dread!"
Said the portly plant with its plump little head.
Together they giggle, rain or shine,
Showing their spirit, oh-so-divine!

In this vibrant patch of playful cheer,
Nature's quirks make magic appear.
So here's to the greens, brightening the day,
With humor and joy, they laugh and sway.

Verdure's Dance in the Sun's Caress

In pots so round, they jiggle and sway,
Chasing the rays, they frolic all day.
With roots so stout, they laugh and tease,
In a world of bright, they're the kings of breeze.

While neighbors pout, they giggle with glee,
Stretching their limbs, is it you, or me?
Charmed by the glow of the warm golden light,
These frolicsome greens bring joy, pure delight.

When shadows creep in, they huddle tight,
Sharing their stories, both silly and bright.
"Oh, did you hear? That cactus tried to dance!"
Yet flopped over sideways, quite caught in a trance!

So raise a glass to our leafy charmers,
With smiles so wide, and antics like farmers.
In this sunny plot, where laughter will thrive,
These verdant pals make us feel so alive.

Sun-Faced Wonders of the Arid Lands

In a barren land, where the sun takes a throne,
These little guys bloom, like they're made of stone.
With a wink and a nod, they tackle the heat,
Sipping up sunshine like a frosty treat.

Their curves and their shapes, they wiggle in style,
Chasing a glimmer, all happy and wile.
"Hey, is that shade?" one sits up to say,
Only to laugh and dance bright away.

In quirky green coats, they banter and joke,
"Did you hear the news? That fern's gone all smoke!"
With a chuckle so loud, they stir up a cheer,
As potted green folk show no trace of fear.

They craft little tales of their sandy abode,
With whispers and giggles, the fun overloads.
In strange little worlds, with the sun as their guide,
They're the jolly green jesters, in nature's wild ride.

Greenery's Glint in Daylight's Hold

In the morning's warmth, they stretch all around,
With leaves full of laughter, they dance on the ground.
"Look at me shine!" the plump ones proclaim,
As they bask in glory, they savor their fame.

One cheeky little plant tells a quirky tale,
Of sunbathing bravely, like a ship's brave sail.
"I've seen it all, from the droplet to day,
And let me tell you, it's all quite okay!"

With a wiggle and shake, they trade leafy news,
"Did you spot that bug? What colorful hues!"
In this pot of fun, every round is a score,
"Quick, scratch that itch, will you cover me more?"

So gather around, for a bright afternoon,
Where every little sprout sings a happy tune.
With glints in their eyes, they lead a parade,
In the garden's glory, all worries do fade.

Blades of Life in Celestial Beams

In a galaxy bright, where the sun sings a song,
These blades of green jive, where they all belong.
Playing tag with light, they stretch out their arms,
Daring the rays to fall for their charms.

"Oh, don't be shy!" squeaks a cactus in glee,
"Join our wacky waltz, oh come dance with me!"
With fluffy tall tops, they twirl and they sway,
In the bright midday sparkle, they light up the play.

Every moment they share, it's a comedic affair,
As one tipsy leaf tries to float on air.
"Is that really me?" it giggles out loud,
As friends burst with laughter, all cheerful and proud.

In this wacky world, under sky-painted beams,
Life's but a jest, or so it seems.
With silly jokes spun, and puns that ignite,
These blades of joy bask in the infinite light.

Gardener's Sunlit Haven

In pots where cacti dance with glee,
A tiny gnome sips minty tea.
Bees buzz in hats, such classy decor,
While lizards play cards right by the door.

Sun has a giggle, shines on the fronds,
And plants tell jokes of their leafy bonds.
Roses wear sunglasses, a stylish flair,
While daisies break out in spontaneous flair.

The gardener chuckles at such a sight,
Her plants are wild, ready to take flight.
With smiles so bright, they sway and sway,
Turning mundane hours into play.

As dusk approaches, they share a grin,
"Who can outgrow the tallest spin?"
Rooftop shenanigans in blooms so bold,
In this sunlit haven, laughter unfolds.

Thorns Among Blossoms

In a patch of color, thorns are found,
They brag of strength; they puff around.
Yellow blooms giggle while pinks keep cool,
"Don't poke the prickles, they play the fool!"

Petals have secrets, they whisper and tease,
Trading wild stories with giggles and wheezes.
Sunbeams roll by, casting light on this jam,
As roses play chess and dahlias scram.

A spiky comedian tells cactus jokes,
While daisies laugh at oblivious folks.
"When you touch a thorn, you might just squeal!"
"Best stick to petals; they won't make you feel."

As twilight approaches, the laughter wanes,
Thorns and blossoms, the best of campaigns.
With every chatter, they bloom with delight,
In this garden realm, humor takes flight.

Prismatic Dreams basking in Gold

In shades of green, a rainbow they weave,
Little plants giggle; oh, they believe.
Ceramic critters sit back and cheer,
While the sun paints gold, they shift into gear.

Cacti compete in a bobbing race,
A lizard high-fives, 'What a wild place!'
Succulent pals flaunt their vibrant hues,
Shadeless and bright, they spread their good news.

The sun has a party, it brings all its rays,
Moss makes confetti, pushing all clichés.
With sparkles that twinkle, they shimmy and sway,
Singing to shadows, "Let's seize the day!"

As twilight spills, dreams dance on the edge,
The plants share snacks, a quirky pledge.
In prismatic glory, they glow in their mold,
Living for laughter, basking in gold.

Alive in the Haze of Warmth

Beneath a sky painted in orange mist,
Plants unite, forming a sunshine twist.
Pots wear sassy smiles, blooms do a jig,
In the haze of warmth, they dance, big and sprig.

Cacti compete for the quirkiest shade,
While petunias gossip about the parade.
Inspecting the soil, they brush off the dirt,
Sharing their tales of sunburn and hurt.

"Don't be a prick!" the daisies all jeer,
While ferns spin tales of not showing fear.
Oh, the drama that brews in this hot little place,
Where each leaf is a character with a bright face.

As evening fades in, they settle with cheer,
"More sun tomorrow! Have no fear!"
Alive in this haze, with laughter they bask,
In warm, silly joys that they can't help but ask.

Glimmers of Life in Dry Earth

In pots they thrive, no need for rain,
Their thirst is low, they can't complain.
A cactus gives a gentle poke,
While I pretend to stay awake, not choke.

With colors bright, they steal the show,
An office desk, a planty glow.
Who needs a garden, big and wide?
When tiny thorns bring joy inside?

When brown thumbs try to keep them neat,
They wave their leaves, a quiet beat.
"Oh look, it's life!" we often croon,
As they laugh at us by the light of the moon.

These little guys, they know the game,
While I just play the watering shame.
Yet still they shine, without a frown,
In this dry land, they're kings, not clowns.

Lush Enclaves of Sun-drenched Beauty

In pots of glory on a shelf,
Each little star laughs at itself.
With cheeky grins, they soak up rays,
While I'm indoors in a sunless haze.

They shimmy proudly with a sway,
"Is it summer?" they seem to say.
While I, the plant-parent, bow in fear,
Luring me into a succulent sphere.

One day I spilled water for a drink,
Now I think they're starting to stink.
With every leaf and every stem,
These crispy pals, my laughter's gem.

In my living room, they form a crew,
As I can't tell what's yellow or blue.
But each little friend brings such delight,
With all their quirks, they shine so bright!

Sunlit Succor for the Soul

Bright green warriors in a row,
With more charm than I could ever show.
In this dry realm, they reign supreme,
While I'm straying from my watering dream.

With clever quips, they make me grin,
"Quench your thirst, we're here to win!"
As I search for my watering can,
They just giggle, "You'll never span."

They sunbathe well with such finesse,
While I tend to create a mess.
"Photosynthesis? It's all the rage!"
While I'm slipping on a dusty stage.

Such funny friends with endless flair,
Each tiny leaf a breath of air.
As I fumble through, they just stay cool,
In their own way, the wisest fools.

Nature's Living Trophies

On my sill, they bask with glee,
"Look at us, the A-list, see?"
They flaunt their hues in merry bands,
While I wrestle with a soil-filled hand.

One day I bought a fancy pot,
Now it's a throne for all that's hot.
While I dream of a garden grand,
These leafy bunches take command.

With every spike and every bloom,
They strut around, filling the room.
"Natural beauty," they smugly claim,
While I print their name and play the game.

In this trophy case, they never wilt,
While I stand by, filled with guilt.
Yet still they cheer me on with grace,
These little wonders, the funniest place!

www.ingramcontent.com/pod-product-compliance
Lightning Source LLC
Chambersburg PA
CBHW070312120526
44590CB00017B/2642